Through the Hands of Time

Stacy Lynn Wilderman

Dennet & Ken,
Happy Reading!
Stacy Wilderman
11/23/06

PublishAmerica
Baltimore

First printing

At the specific preference of the author, PublishAmerica allowed this work to remain exactly as the author intended, verbatim, without editorial input.

ISBN: 1-4241-1690-2
PUBLISHED BY PUBLISHAMERICA, LLLP
www.publishamerica.com
Baltimore

Printed in the United States of America

Dedicated to:

My parents, sister and family,
Grandmothers

Especially to my Grandfather Czirjak, thank you
for your encouragement

Acknowledgements:

Thank you to the numerous people who have come
into my life that I was able to write a poem about.
Without you in my life, there would have been no
poem.

Thank you to Foothills Composite High School for
starting a poetry book in 1991. It was because of you
that I started to write. Without you this book would
not have been possible.

MEMORIAL

FOR THE LOVE OF ONE
(Andrew Czirjak's Memorial, July 31, 1999)

For the love of one, we gather together,
To pay our respect for the one that has passed away.

For the love of one we remember how he was:
Playful,
Interested in what you did,
Strong,
A man not abundance in words but you knew he cared
by a look,
A traveler,
A father, a brother,
A husband and a grandfather.

For the love one we remember the good and the bad,
Going through the sad and the glad.
We remember birthdays and Christmases, family
outings, and grand occasions.
For the love of one we look at our pictures and
remember.

For the love of one we will never forget, as we don't
want him to disappear from our hearts.
For the love of one should always be close to our
hearts, month after month, and year after year.
For the love of one, we will always remember.

FAMILY

OUR FAMILY ALBUM

When I'm feeling sad or blue
I like to go fetch our family album.
For it will have many wonderful pictures
From our past and to the present.

There are birthday celebrations,
Christmas and New Years fun,
Halloween and Easter pictures,
And travel enjoyment as a family.

When there are others around.
It's fun to reminisce about the old days,
Have a few good laughs at the present,
And remember those days of the few future pictures
that you have just recently taken.

Whether you have had good times or bad
You can enjoy your pictures that you've collected,
Forgive one another, as you only get one family.
All this emotion comes from looking through our
family album.

FAMILY TIES

We are bound together
Even though at times we wish we weren't.
You get to know one another
And you know each other's pit falls.

The siblings play and laugh together,
They fight and bicker together,
Take sides with one another,
And occasionally need adult supervision.

The adults talk amongst themselves.
They talk about work,
They gossip a little,
And wonder how other relatives are doing.

You travel together to distance places.
Enjoying each other's company,
Seeing historical sites,
And being together as a family.

Whatever happens between your family
Whether it's good or bad
You can bet that you are going through them together,
For that is what family ties are all about.

WHAT OUR ANCESTORS DID

Many come from the old country
To make a life in the new one.
They came alone or as a married couple
Their families were still at home.

They made a new start.
A few of them inquired land.
Upon the land they built a new home
And managed to start a farm.

Work was hard for many.
For they worked from dawn to dusk,
Tending to the field with back breaking work.
Hoping their animals survived.

Sometimes the land was plentiful
With lots of food to eat.
At other times the land was barren
And there was very little to carry on during the winter.

Many worked in the town.
Labor jobs were plentiful with very little pay.
Some got hurt or died doing dangerous work,
Which left many children parentless.

Town life were joyful times
Many gossiped about others.
There were always things to do in town
Whether it was good or sinful.

In a small rural community
Everyone knew everyone else.
Which was sometimes either good or bad
Depending on your point of view.

Whatever happened in those crazy Wild West days,
When times were hard but in the end a joyful life.
History was being created for us
By what our ancestors did.

LIKE MOTHER

There is no one as special
Then having a Grandmother.
For she takes care of you, scolds you and loves you
Like a mother.

Like mother
She is gentle,
Has good advice that you can listen to,
She is happy to see you and happy to see you go.
All the while letting you know she loves you.

When you were little and you stayed with her
She took care of you when you were sick.
Sat up nights when you had a bad dream and couldn't
sleep.
Talked with you and answered your million questions.
She did all these things just as a mother would.

Now you are older and so is your Grandmother.
She isn't taking care of you so much
But you are taking care of her.
Just like you have to do for your mother, she is doing
the same.

One can't help but notice
How two people who are the same can be different.
No matter how you are born
Eventually you will do everything like mother.

NOTHING BUT LOVE

There is nothing so pure
Than the love that surrounds you
For from that love has formed
A bond that remains unbroken.

God chose us to become a family
Because of the love and laughter that we would share
He knew that we'd remain together
Until the very end of time.

With His blessing's and guidance
We've grown by leaps and bounds.
For He knows that there is nothing so magical
Than the presence of little ones.

No matter where you go or what you do
Somewhere there is a place called home
That shows nothing but love
To bring you all together.

CHILDREN

A MIRACLE

A baby is truly a miracle.
For once you have one,
You don't want to let them go,
As you love and cherish it so much.

As the years go by
And your baby gets bigger.
You come to realize how it came into your world
And the memories will make you smile.

If we never have miracles,
This world would be a dull place.
As only miracles brighten up your life
And make each day so special.

We all hope that you and this miracle,
Turn out well for the better.
That you never forget the friendship,
That so many of us have given you.

We wish you good luck for the future
And hope the miracle is as bright as the sun.
For your miracle will remind you
That you were glad you had made that choice.

AN ADDED ADDITION
(Dedicated to Erin and Chad Niemans)

A little biddy baby
Is starting to grow.
We're anxiously waiting for the day
When he or she is born.

Excitement starts to build,
As you prepare for the many changes.
From carriages to high chairs, clothes and toys.
Whoever thought a baby could use so much.

This baby will be so loved
Not just because it's the first,
But, there are family member's waiting
To love it with all of their heart.

Sometime next year in 2002,
We will be celebrating the big day.
Waiting for a small little bundle of joy
To become an added addition.

SPECIAL DELIVERY

On July 18, 2002,
Treyton Andrew Niemans was born
To a proud Mama and Papa,
Who anxiously waited for your arrival.

For nine long months
We had waited for you.
Our love for you growing stronger
As each day passed.

As soon as we met you
For the very first time,
We realized that our love for you
Is always going to be there.

There is nothing so magical
Than to witness a miracle
And knowing that what appears
In the end is a special delivery.

WATCHING OVER YOU
(Dedicated to Treyton Niemans)

There are little words to express
This love that I have for you
For you are my bright spot
In a world that seems to drag me down.

You make my heart sing
Every time that I see you.
Your laughter and your smile,
Pulls me out of this darkness that I seem to be in.

You are like a ray of light
That shines upon me.
Just the smallest gesture given by you
Makes the darkness goes away.

As I watch you grow,
My memories will be plentiful,
Because for everything that happens to you
It will happen as I am watching over you.

A BUNDLE OF JOY

How do I describe these feelings?
That seem to rain down upon me.
Because every time I look at you,
You fill my heart with happiness.

You are a ray of sunshine
That brightens up any room.
For those long beams of warmth
Touch down to my very soul.

You lift me up when I'm down
You bring warmth to my heart.
And every time I see your face,
Brings a smile to mine.

You will always be in my heart
Since the very first time that I saw you
No matter whatever happens
You will always remain my little bundle of joy.

ALL I ASK OF YOU
(Dedicated to Chase Niemans)

Whenever I gaze upon your face
You uplift my soul to Heaven
Because seeing that happy smile
Brightens up any mood I may be in.

Nothing gives me pleasure
Than knowing when I look at you
Your eyes light up each time
When you recognize the one that you love.

I hope that nothing changes
Once you've continued to grow,
That the smile that you've had as a babe
Continues on till the end of time.

Whatever changes may come our way
One thing I hope will stay
Our love for one another will never stray.
That is all that I ask of you.

SO MUCH LOVE
(Dedicated to the newest Niemans)

An exciting new adventure
Is starting to grow
For within the next year
A bundle of joy will be born.

A little biddy baby
That will be added to the two
Who knows what it could be
A boy or a girl?

Nothing could be sweeter
Than the love that has surrounded you
Because you know that each child
Will return that love times three.

With so much love
That has radiated between you
Your little family has grown
By the grace of God's love.

FRIENDSHIP

BEST FRIENDS

We are best friends, yes it's true.
I tell you my secrets,
You tell me yours too.
It's a bond no one can break!

Others will try and break us,
But we stick together like glue.
No one is a better friend,
Then you!

Whatever my problems,
Whatever my sorrows,
Whatever my worries,
You are listening to me.

You give me comfort and understanding,
When I need a person to listen.
You will be by my side,
Showing encouragement and love.

I hope you'll always be my friend,
However far or near we are.
And keep our friendship as close as possible,
No matter how old we are!

ALONG CAME YOU

When I was feeling blue,
And didn't know where to turn.
Along came you
To brighten up my day and make it better.

When there was no one to talk to
And no one to listen.
Along came you
To help me when I needed it.

However far or near I am
When no one is there.
Along came you
To be my friend.

Whenever I need someone
When it seems there is no one in my life.
At least on thing I know for sure
Along came you to be there.

FRIENDSHIP BY A LETTER

Two strangers like us
Met by letter.
Each from a different country,
Managing to be friends
By writing each other letters.

It started with an introduction,
Followed by the beginning.
We've come to the middle
But so far haven't come to the end.

We've gone by the postal system.
Neither rain nor sleet nor snow,
Our letters have always gone through.
Although now that is known as snail mail.

Today no matter where we are,
We can reach each other by e-mail,
Which has helped us keep in touch,
For someone had always been slower than snail mail.

No matter which way we've written,
We've managed to stay friends.
We've listened to each other complain,
Known each other's pain,
And have known each other's happiness.

What has surprised me the most.
Is that all of this just started by a letter.
Through the lines of blank paper,
We have created a friendship by letter.

UNTIL WE MEET AGAIN

Very few people whom you meet become friends.
There are still those few that do become the best.
You were my friend from the first day,
Until the very last day.

You knew my hopes, my dreams.
Whom I wanted to fall in love with.
We talked about everything.
We even had laughter and shed a few tears.
You were the one always by my side and I yours.

No one knew me as well as you did,
Even though others will come after to try.
Life will be very dull,
Without having you in mine.

You will always be my friend,
Wherever I go, whatever I do.
Until the day comes, when I'm old and grey,
We will meet again.

A SHOULDER TO LEAN ON

Whatever is troubling you,
Whenever you are feeling blue,
When the world has gotten you feeling crazy,
You have a shoulder to lean on.

When you're looking for a sympathetic ear,
When you feel like you don't have a friend that cares,
When you feel lost and scared,
You have a shoulder to lean on.

If you feel life is steering you down the wrong path,
And you seem bewildered and confused.
Whenever you feel you need some assurance,
You have a shoulder to lean on.

Whatever problems or concerns you may have,
Whatever feelings you may be experiencing at that
moment.
You can always count on me,
For I'll give you a shoulder to lean on.

IT'S WHAT'S ON THE INSIDE THAT COUNTS

It doesn't matter how we dress,
It doesn't matter how we look,
It doesn't matter what we do,
It just matters how we feel about ourselves.

It matters that you try,
It matters that you don't give up,
It matters that you did your best,
To get the accomplishments done.

It matters that we treat one another with respect,
It matters that we love one another,
It matters that we all get along,
For no one should be treated differently.

When we take a look inside ourselves
We can see into our soul.
And no one can tell you anything differently
For it's what's on the inside that counts.

INSPIRATION

DIVINE INSPIRATION

When life steers you down the wrong path
It can sometimes feel as if you will never see daylight
again.
For when you least expect it,
Someone comes to change your perspective on life.

You don't know who that person will be.
They could be family,
They could be friends,
They could be a complete stranger.

By showing you love and concern,
Pushing you at times when you feel you can't go
further,
Always being by your side.
This will be the best medicine anyone could receive.

However confusing life may be
And you're not sure where to turn.
God listens by giving guidance and love
In the end, all of these things could be your divine
inspiration.

DAWNING OF A NEW DAY

With outstretched hands
You beckon me to You
To be brought into the fold of Your flock,
By the radiance and warmth of Your love.

All my cares, concerns, and worries,
Are blown away into the wind.
Because I know that Your love,
Outshines any problems that may plague me.

From the slightest touch of an angel's wing.
I know that You are there
Protecting me and guiding me
Through life's ever present battles.

Knowing that my thoughts are completely Yours,
Forcing me out of the darkness and into the light.
And by the dawning of a new day,
You make new beginnings happen when we believe.

NEVER WITHOUT YOU

Your praises have been sung
By a powerful written word,
That uplifts my soul to Heaven
Though Your light shines down on me.

No one speaks to me the way that You do.
Your voice will always be in harmony with mine
And every little echo that I hear
Tells me that You are never very far away.

Whatever my heart may feel
I know that Your presence is there.
Because the strength of Your love
Is a shroud that is always surrounding me.

With each little step that I take,
I am learning to walk in Your ways.
As I continue to move towards You,
I will always realize that I am never without You.

AN OPEN HEART

By the grace of Your love
I feel Your heart beating,
As one with my own
For You are alive within me.

Knowing that I am walking in Your footsteps
Gives me the strength and hope
To continue moving forward
From the darkness into the light.

If there is ever any doubt
I realize that all I need to do,
Is look towards You
Because Your guidance never steers me wrong.

What You have done for me
I will be forever grateful
For You have made me see
That a closed heart can become an open heart.

JUST BETWEEN YOU AND I

No other soul shall know
My very thoughts, my secrets, or my pain.
Only one shall know everything
And that someone is You.

You are my knight in shinning armour.
You are my hope when there is none.
You are my light when it is dark.
And You are my salvation when the time has come.

Like an eagle soaring high above the earth,
My soul gets lifted just as high
Because my heart is filled with happiness
By the very thought of You.

Whenever I have times of distress,
I believe that whatever has been said,
Will never be moved from Your lips.
For whatever I have prayed will be just between You
and I.

NO MORE WANDERING

My feet have not been idle,
Since the day You came into my life.
You've opened up a whole new world to me,
Which with my eyes closed, I could not see.

You have brought peace and harmony
Within these four walls of misery.
What was once dark and foreboding
Now shines with rays of light.

Your presence I feel is near
Your heart beats in time with mine.
And with your outstretched hands
You're guiding me to a better life.

What has once been idle,
Now has become silent once more.
For I know I don't have to look
No further because I wander no more.

NOTHING COMPARED TO YOU

Never did I dream
That you'd walk into my life
For your protective shroud
Shines like a light raining down on me.

From the slightest touch of an angel's kiss
I know that you are near
Protecting me and guiding me
Through life's ever present problems.

In a world full of confusion
You are like a steady rock
In which a person can rely on
Throughout the rest of their days.

There's nothing compared to you
Since you've become a part of my life
For I know that you are my best friend
And there is nothing more that I need.

RUNNING TOWARDS YOU

No matter whatever challenges may bring
You know that there is a place
Where one can unburden their problems
And eventually uplift their soul.

It is a place where one can find
You're loving arms guiding them in
Making them feel safe and comforted
In a house where they know You are.

Love can be felt
As soon as you walk through the door
For You make them feel lighthearted
Whenever they come to gather.

Because they run towards You
They know that they will come home
To a place where they can be near
Your loving guidance for all eternity.

ROMANCE

DREAMING OF YOU

I'm dreaming of you,
As I see us walking hand in hand.
Down that lonely beach.
Wondering if you love me like I love you.

I wish I could figure out your feelings,
I wish I knew mine too.
Everyday is better when we're not apart,
But as soon as we are, it's a dark spot in my heart.

You turn to kiss me,
And my heart flutters so.
I realize I should have no worries,
As I understand how much you love and need me like I
need you.

If we should ever part,
I hope you don't leave me with a broken heart.
I will always love you as if you were standing next to me
And holding me as close to you are you are now.

I hope my dreams never end.
I hope they never die.
I hope they will flutter out of the dark spot,
And into the sunlight that you are standing in.

FROM MY HEART

Everything is so confusing,
I have no idea what to do.
I see you from a distance
And I know I love you so.

I hope I can tell you,
What's been on my mind?
But I fear you'll laugh
And go further away from me as you already are.

It's not easy for me to tell you
The things I'd like to say.
But if you'd only knew the love
That is coming from my heart.

Every heartbeat,
Every moment,
Every kiss I see you give me,
All this comes from my heart.

I don't know when
And I don't know how.
I'll be able to say
These words I've wanted to say.

That one day I hope you'll listen
And one day I hope you will see.
That when I say I love you,
It's all coming from my heart.

IN A MOMENT

So many things that I want to say
But I just can't find the words.
You're never around to listen
Because you can't be near.

If only you could steal a minute,
Do you realize how much time?
You'd get to say all the things
That you can only say in a moment.

This is all so new and exciting,
My life has turned for the better.
That's because you're next to me
Even if only it was for a moment.

I don't know what I'd have done
If you did not show up when you did.
You could have walked by,
But you stayed for just a moment.

You are so dear to me
I can't tell you how much you mean to me.
The only things I know is
That all this happened with in a moment.

UNTAMED HEART

My heart has been restless
For it's always been on the run.
Until the day that you walked into my life
And made me whole again.

You sang me love songs
That has a honky-tonk melody.
Each song promising to
Love me with all of your heart.

You tell me to have no worries
For our love will always be strong,
And it will never be untamed
Like the land that is always changing.

I feel a sense of calmness
And relax in your strong and comfortable arms.
For I now know that I am safe and happy,
Since you have tamed my broken heart.

UNTIL NOW

Until now you have been a dream
One that keeps playing in my head all the time.
So many details seem real
That I can't believe it was only a dream.

Until now I never knew what love felt like.
A kiss was just an imagination.
Holding hands were just part of my thoughts.
Being content with one another was impossible.

Until now I never had anyone like you.
You love me for who I am.
Never judging me as those in my dreams do.
We always have good times together.

Until now I had felt alone
But you came into my life
Making me feel free
Where, until now, you were only an image.

BETWEEN THE LINES

I don't understand these signals
That I keep getting from you
For you have expressed little words
To this broken heart of mine.

Nothing is the same anymore
Especially your love for me.
You keep slipping away
From my outstretched hands.

I never did think that you'd hurt me
Because I thought we were strong
To stand through the pain together
But you've proven me wrong.

Reading between the lines I've seen
A relationship falling apart
Because two souls have become one
Since we two have bid one another farewell.

CLOSE TO YOU

My heart has not stopped beating
Since the day you walked into my life
For you brought a flood of happiness
To this weary soul of mine.

Love blossomed since the day that I met you
With each passing day
It keeps growing stronger
To form this bond that we now share.

There is nothing sweeter
Than that promised first kiss
Because heat is sent down to my toes
And they have been tingling ever since.

Becoming this close to you
Has made me open up my eyes
That even though trust was once broken
You made it possible to believe in love once again.

WAITING FOR LOVE

From the first day that I met you
You made my heart skip a tiny beat
For the friendship that has formed
Has slowly been blossoming into love.

With each passing day it grows stronger
To fill me up with happiness.
At the end of the long day
Your face is the one I want to see.

The time that is spent together
Has blessed me in so many ways
Because you've made me see
That you are the one for always.

Expressing my very thoughts to you
Fills me with absolute dread
Since I'm not so sure
That you are waiting for love the same as I.

ANNIVERSARY

HOW FAR WE HAVE COME

A new sunrise to show the day.
Today is the big day; it's your 30th anniversary!
You look over at your wife and can't believe how far
you have come together.
Was it only 30 years ago when you both said, "I do?"

You remember the day:
Filled with excitement,
Nervousness,
The pride you both felt when you looked at one
another.
You couldn't believe how lucky you felt that you
caught the other.

After the big day, you're life started:
A family joined the ranks.
First the oldest was born then the youngest.
After that there were no more.
When they got older you thought:
"Thank God!"

Miraculously they grew and left home.
One got married,
The other is still thinking about it.
You became just two again.
Some days that is good, other days that is bad.
No matter what happens, you know you love one
another.

Thinking about the future,
Thinking about the past,
And thinking about the present,
You can't believe how far you have come.
The only thing that matters is the precious memories
you made,
When that big day came when you both said, "I do."

THOSE SPECIAL MOMENTS
(Dedicated to Erin and Chad)

We have only been together for a year
But those are my happiest memories.
For it was only at this time last year,
When you decided to be in my life forever.

On the day we said, "I do"
You looked like a wonderful angel,
And I was so happy
I had managed to catch you before you were gone.

Each day has brought new discoveries.
We laugh and talk,
We enjoy our togetherness,
And we have gotten to know one another better.

You have brought such great joy to my heart
That no matter what else comes along,
I'll be happy to know that we are doing them together.
And those will be my special moments.

ON YOUR GOLDEN ANNIVERSARY
(Dedicated to Doug and Belva Knox)

From the moment that you first met
You knew that you were going to be together
For love has withstood the hands of time
When you said those important words "I do".

Though the many years have come and gone
Your memories will always hold a place in your heart
Because you know that you did them together
And that precious gift is worth holding on to.

Every day brought new discoveries
As you followed your own path
For they added both joy and sorrow
To an already blessed life.

Everything that you have meant to one another
Is being celebrated with joy on this day
For there is no love as great as the one that you share
Than on your golden anniversary.

DEDICATED TO

SISTERS
(Dedicated to my sister, Erin)

Some come in three, fours, fives, or even more.
But we came together as two.
Which is just as well,
For one is better for me than having none at all.

Fate brought us together,
There were times when I cried out,
"Dear God, why?"
Although no answer would come to me.

You were my ache and pain,
As I was yours.
But somehow we managed to be there for one another,
Which I'm sure makes Mom and Dad proud.

At least times have changed (Thank God!)
For you are headed down a journey,
That I am happy you are.
This way you can help me with mine.

No matter what changes occur,
You are always going to be my sister,
And for that I am thankful for.
For there is no better sister for me than you.

IN OTHER WORDS
(Erin and Chad's wedding, December 18, 1999)

When we met, we were in high school,
Just two lost souls waiting to meet each other.
In other words, we met by chance.

We became friends.
How? I'll never know.
In other words, our friendship put us to the test.

We graduated, grew apart, and then reunited.
In other words, that reunion brought us closer.

I knew of my love for you,
You knew of your love for me.
In other words, we both realized at the same time that
we loved each other.

You and I became a team:
We laughed and cried,
We knew what the other was thinking,
We talked of our dreams,
And we went places together.
In other words, you are the brightest spot in my life.

You are my soul, my life,
My home, my dream, my partner,
My friend and my other half.
In other words, we will be together until the end.

TO THE ONE I LOVE
(Dedicated to Stuart)

To the one I love I thank you:
You're with me through the good and the bad.
You comfort me when I'm upset,
You cheer me up when I'm down.
You're always there to cheer me on.
For all these things I'm thankful your there when you
are.

To the one I love I see our past:
Hanging out,
Enjoying each other's company.
Being friends before we became lovers.
Seeing you standing by my side as always.

To the one I love I see our future:
Happiness at being husband and wife.
Watching our children grow,
Seeing our grandchildren grow,
And being together as a family.
Our senior years will be filled with fun and joy.

To the one I love I know you're always there.
You've made me happy and you've made me mad.
No one can argue that you are the best person for me,
And the one that I am happy you are in my life forever.

SOMETHING ABOUT YOU
(Dedicated to Stuart)

There's something about you
That makes my heart flutter.
You make me happy,
My heart sings when I see you.

Something about you
Shows me there's no boundaries.
You've got my heart,
And I know I've got yours.
Together we are sharing a heart as one.

There's something about you
That makes me excited,
That makes me feel special,
That makes me know you are mine.
You show me how you care in your own ways.

Something about you
Fits me like a glove,
That feels like a good worn shoe,
That's comfortable as old clothes.
You fit in my life so well.

There's something about you
That lets me know you are there for always,
Through thick and thin,
No matter what problems may arise between us.
All I'm happy to know is that you love me whatever happens,
And to know that makes me happy that we are
together forever.

SOMEONE TO WATCH OVER US
(Dedicated to my Grandpa)

You were sent away from us
When we needed you the most.
This sad feeling has been in our hearts
Ever since you passed away last year.

We have grieved for you,
We have missed you,
We've remembered all of our good memories,
Which for us is one way of keeping your memory alive.

You were sent here on this Earth
To watch and take care of our family.
You saw us through
The happy moments and through the saddest.

Now you have been sent to Heaven
To become a guardian angel.
Every now and then God sends you down,
As someone to watch over us.

LIKE NO ONE ELSE
(Dedicated to my mother)

With a steady and strong hand
To guide you from life's many mysteries.
A soft voice explaining all
When you feel you have one too many woes.

A comfortable shoulder to lean on
When you have many tears to shed.
Someone who understand all the trials you have gone
through,
For she has done them herself.

A sympathetic ear
Listening to all your troubles and wonderful times.
Giving you advice when you need it
And sometimes giving you advice when you don't.

A woman with a strong voice
Whom you can listen to,
Whom you can trust never to take you down the
wrong path,
For her advice is worth more than gold.

There is no one quite like a mother
For she is the one who is with you at all times,
Cares and loves you for who you are.
Only your mother can do this like no one else.

UNCONDITIONAL LOVE
(Dedicated to my father)

When you were very young
You remember being in father's arms.
Those long arms cradling you
Knowing you felt safe and loved.

In father's arms
You listened to many bedtime stories,
Enjoyed a good tickle,
And received little Eskimo kisses.

In father's arms
You cried when you were hurt,
Feeling safe from the pain,
And enjoyed his love and concern.

In father's arms
You said goodbye.
When you went away to college
And eventually got married.

No matter if you are young or old,
You can always find a safe haven.
Knowing that inside your father's arms,
You are finding unconditional love.

WITH LOVE
(Dedicated to my Grannie, on her birthday)

There is nothing more precious
Than receiving a gift from a loved one
Knowing that they thought of you.
The joy you felt when you received it.

Remembering all the past presents,
The cards written to you,
Your presence at family functions
Just knowing you are there means so much.

What I'll always remember the most
Is that whatever was given
At the end of the card or gift tag
Was written with these words, "With Love."

Those words mean the most
For it showed that you loved
Each and every person
That was brought into your life.

Today on your special day
I have written this poem for you
To show you as you've shown me
That at the end will be written, "With Love."

PRECIOUS MEMORIES
(Dedicated to my Grandmother)

Memories of yesteryear
Flash through my mind.
Each one more precious
Than the one before.

Remembering the laughter,
Remembering the tears,
Remembering the thoughtful times,
Remembering the quiet times.

All that has been taught to me
Was done with love and care.
All that I've learned from you
Will stay with me forever.

Our time spent together
Has been one in a million
For our love for one another will stay
And that will be my precious memory.

MY LIFE AS A CAT
(Dedicated to Casey Wilderman)

I joined a family who lived on a farm
My life was perfect, complete,
And I was in awe.
Everything a cat could ask for was here.

I could lie all over the furniture,
Except when they caught me.
There were other times when they didn't
And I felt so giddy (He! He!)

I enjoyed going out and coming in,
Going out and coming in.
Rolling in gravel making my fur all dusty.
The barn became my second home when they were away.

When I arrived there were four.
One moved out and came back.
The other moved out and came back.
Then there was just two.

Food became my passion.
I loved peanuts and popcorn,
The nuts and bolts at Xmas,
And anything that dropped on the floor while they
were cooking.

I enjoyed a good lap
When I could find one.
For it brought me nothing but happiness
When they made my motor roar.

My life as a cat has been complete.
For God has decided to take me away
To live a peaceful life without any sickness or pain.
But I will never forget those whom loved and cared for
me.

ON THIS SPECIAL OCCASION
(Dedicated to my sister Erin)

Thirty years ago today,
On May 14, 1975,
A beautiful baby
Was born to proud and happy parents.

They watched you grow
Into a confident young woman
Who completed what she set out to do
In all of her accomplishments.

They walked you down the aisle
To a man who was waiting to love you forever.
And from that love formed
The greatest treasures you could ever hold.

Today we are celebrating
A milestone that you have reached,
For on this special occasion,
Nothing matters than being with family and friends.

NATURE

THUNDERSTORM

A howling wind,
A beat of a drum,
A flash in the sky,
Clouds coming in closer.

All of a sudden torrent rain comes down,
Coming down harder, harder, and harder.
The beat of a drum becomes louder, louder, and louder.
The flash in the sky seems as if it is taking your picture.

Some rain falls hard and some falls soft,
Some rain falls slow and some falls fast.
These are all the different types of rain.
But none can beat a thunderstorm.

It's got its own style,
That people do notice.
And when the thunderstorm is over,
The world is the most beautiful place you've ever seen.

Grass is wet with dew and greener then ever before.
Trees stand tall and green.
A thunderstorm is good you see,
For it gives beautiful things we love best,
A chance to grow, to be seen, and most of all to stay.

BLUEBIRD'S SONG

I heard a bluebird sing
One gorgeous spring day.
It had a sweet melody
That anyone can hear.

The bluebird sits on a branch
In the weeping willow tree.
From dusk until sunset
That is his home.

When fall comes
My bluebird leaves.
I don't get to hear him sing,
Until spring comes again.

The bluebird was born here
And I watched the family grow.
The parents taught him to fly
Then when winter came they flew away.

I hope my bluebird never leaves
For it returns every spring.
When I hear the bluebird's lovely singing
I am renewed with a sense of hope and joy.

IN THE FIELD OF GOLD

Standing together two by two
We watch the sun go down
Hitting the field of wheat,
To make it look like gold.

We are peaceful and serene
Letting the hectic day go by
Without a care in the world,
Standing in the field of gold.

The wind has died down from the day
And a quiet breeze is blowing.
The wheat sound like a soft ocean breeze
That is making us drowsy with sleep.

The quiet bussing of bugs,
The chirping song of the birds,
And the croaking of frogs by the lake,
Are reminding us that nature is still a mystery.

One can't help but notice
How human and nature can immerge together
Quietly accepting one another as they are.
All of this happens while standing in a field of gold.

FROM DAWN TO DUSK

In the early morning light,
Nature stirs us awake.
Making us long for the day
And what it could bring.

Another new day
To keep us busy with work.
From task to task
It seems as if we are never done.

The young at heart are busy learning and are at play,
The adults groan with a mountain of work before them,
The elders are busy talking about the old days.
People are doing their best to appreciate life.

Eventually everything winds down.
From the young to the very old, get together
To enjoy the peace and harmony amongst themselves.
This is how we all get along.

No matter what the days bring
All of us should remember how precious life is.
For another one does not come along once we are done,
As God has decided that what happens in-between
only goes from dawn to dusk.

PRAIRIE SONG

Each morning at sunrise
I can hear the birds starting to chirp
Letting me know that it is time,
To get up and start the day.

The cows in the field
Bellow out their greeting.
To let me know that they are there,
Waiting to be feed and to be noticed.

All day long you can hear
The talk of the water foul
And the croaking of frogs.
Letting me know that the prairie is always changing.

When night comes
You can hear the coyotes howling.
Their song echoes throughout the land,
Giving me a sense of comfort and safety.

One thing I know for sure
Is that I don't need to listen to a top twenty tune.
For whatever music I hear comes from the prairie land,
And it's signing my favorite song.

HOME IS WHERE YOUR HEART IS

From the Rocky Mountains
To the rolling foothills.
From the lush prairie fields
To the city skyscrapers.

From the quietness of the prairies.
The smell of fresh air
The wind blowing through the trees.
Nature becoming one with the land.

To the city with busy streets
The people are constantly on the go.
The sights that are a wonder to be hold.
A city skyline that can be seen for miles.

From the ranchlands of the foothills
With cattle grazing the land.
Trees stand as tall as skyscrapers here.
The mountains show a breath taking view.

To the Rocky Mountains
Its terrain not quite the same.
Nature is very unforgiving,
As she changes the faces every day.

Wherever you live,
From the Rocky Mountains to the rolling foothills,
From the lush prairie fields to the city skyscrapers,
Home is where your heart is.

WINTER

Dull, boring and cold
This is what winter is to me.
The sun barley shines,
As it hides behind the clouds.

White all around
With snow drifts as high as mountains.
You shovel and shovel never getting rid of it,
You finally think, "Oh well!"

Winter sports pop up.
With hockey, skating, and skiing.
Winter festivals and parties
Are to mark happy occasions.

When warm weather comes around
That's where I'm the happiest.
As it's a sign that spring is closer
And the dullness of winter soon over!

WONDERS OF SPRING

Out of the depths of winter's cold
Where nights are long and days are short.
The land is blanketed with snow
To make all life want to stay indoors.

At a certain time of year
The air becomes warmer,
The sun becomes closer to the Earth,
Life and growth start to take shape from the long
winter sleep.

Love starts to blossom
Between the humans and also the animals.
With the wonderment of spring
Anything can happen.

Days are longer and nights are shorter
No one wants to stay inside
For there is always something that you want to do.
Let your imagination run wild.

With the wonders of spring
Come the enjoyment of summer.
The seasons change, never staying the same.
Which still leaves nature a mystery.

BY THE LIGHT OF THE MOON

Whenever I am trouble or feeling blue,
I will stop whatever I may be doing
And will look upwards to the heavens.

Your silvery waves of light shine down on me,
Which makes my heart skip a tiny beat,
For I know that you are watching over me.

You are like a beacon that flashes its light
Protecting me and giving me strength
Threw even the darkest of nights.

No matter what problems I may be facing,
Or what fears I may be fighting, I will know
That by the light of the moon they will disappear.

MISCELLANOUS

BOX OF CARDS

Looking through my box of cards
One can't help but notice
How much a person has grown
By looking at each card through the years.

There are birthdays and Christmases,
There's valentines and Easter.
Many thank you have been received
For that special gift you sent.

Some cards are silly
Some cards are sentimental.
There are cards given by family
And there are cards given by friends.

Whatever memories I have
By looking at each card
I know that they were sent
By people who loved and knew you the best.

CHANCES ARE

Chances are that if the skies are grey,
Eventually they will become blue.

Chances are that if you feel burdened,
There is always a friend willing to listen.

Chances are that if the road looks bumpy and rough,
One knows that a smooth ride is eventually coming.

Chances are that if at times you feel under the weather,
Someone comes along to brighten your day.

Chances are that if you feel like giving up,
Someone somewhere is feeling the same as you.

Chances are that no matter how busy you are,
Things will eventually calm down.

Chances are that if someone is dying today,
Someone somewhere is being born.

Chances are that if you have done a good deed today,
It will eventually be paid back ten-fold.

Chances are that if you spend time with your family,
You might learn something that you never knew before.

Chances are that whatever comes and goes,
Life continues on.

Chances are that no matter how bleak life may look,
Always remember to look at the bright side of life!

CITY OF LIGHTS

City of lights
What you do to me.
I revel in your excitement
That you show every day.

City of lights the history you have.
With your grand churches,
Wonderful art museums,
And sensational gourmet restaurants.

City of lights I love your Parisian ways.
How the language sounds,
How exotic you dress,
And how you open your arms.

City of lights
You have everything that everyone wants.
However, only you can give
That exoticness you do so well.

FORTUNE TELLER

A lonely woman sits on the corner
Holding out her cup and she has a sign
A dollar to tell your fortune.
I go by her every day and always see someone sitting there,
Wanting their fortune told.

I've never wanted my fortune told,
Although someone insisted I have one.
To me they are all nonsense.
My friend had her fortune told and she said it has been
right up till now.
All I did was pooh pooh and avoided the day.

One day the woman called to me after I crossed the street.
I walked over to her without knowing why,
I guess for some reason she pulled me to her.
She grabbed my hand and told me what she saw.
I couldn't see what she did.

While she was telling my fortune, I looked at her.
I think I knew why there were so many people always there.
When you looked at her face it was so grandmotherly
That you felt at ease with her.

After that day I always stopped to talk to her.
She was always happy that I did.
One day I met someone that changed me
And that was what my fortuneteller told me.
I fell in love with him and he met my fortuneteller.
She told us that we were going to be very happy.

We left that day knowing what was ahead of us.
One day we got married and we had moved.
We never saw much of our fortuneteller.
Years later we walked by the same place but no
fortuneteller was there.

We felt sad and wanted her to see how happy we were.
For some reason I felt her presence
And to this day I believe that she is looking down on us.
Knowing that made her all the more special,
For she showed kindness to everyone
Even though she was just a lonely women who told
fortunes on the street.

GRADUATION

Saying goodbye to old friends,
Saying goodbye to the memories,
And the moments you wished you never had.
Saying hello to the new ones.

One night to enjoy your memories
One night to enjoy your friends.
For knowing you might never see each other again,
But living in one another's hearts.

Reach for your dreams,
Reach for the stars.
Never let opportunities pass you by,
For you have only got one chance.

Congratulations Graduate,
You've finally made it!
Make this night,
One of the best you've ever had!

HOME SWEET HOME

There may be no picket fence.
There may be no grass of green.
There may be no flowers blooming.
There may be no big backyard.

There is no grass to mow.
There is no snow to shovel.
There is no backbreaking work
Only lazy days ahead to spend in the sun.

There is a wonderful view
That was hand picked with care.
For no matter which way you look,
You always receive a new surprise.

There are so many wonderful things
Because they were done with love
And to give to someone like me is a great gift to have.
One thing I know for sure is that I'll enjoy my new
home sweet home.

HOMEWORK

Why do teachers do it?
Giving us homework each and every night.
Demands, pressures, deadlines.
It's just too much.
I'm surprised none of us has cracked!

One night I didn't do my homework.
"Where's your homework?" the teacher asked me.
"It seemed to jump into space when I walked to school,"
That seemed a perfect excuse.
Of course the teacher didn't believe it.
And gave me a lesson I would never forget.

I walked out feeling ashamed,
And feeling kind of down.
I wondered what I could do.
I thought and thought and got an idea.
I did my homework that night, determining to do a
good job.

The next day I handed it in, and did such a good job.
But I'll never understand and never want to know why.
It's something we have to put up with,
That has to be done each and every night.

JOURNEYS

From the beginning of time
When the world was new
And innocence was not lost
A piece of history was born.

Nothing could have prepared you
For the great love that you found
Because what formed from that love
Came the greatest treasure that you possessed.

Though the many years have passed you by
Your memories will always hold a place in your heart
As year after year and month after month
Your blessed life will be one to hold on to.

Everything that has come your way
Has been guided by a strong presence
And by the will of faith and love
Your journey will end by the light of Heaven.

LOST INNOCENCE

The world has changed forever
During one September morning in 2001,
Shaking a nation to its knees
By a destructive and senseless act.

Many innocent lives were lost
With many relatives praying for the return of loved ones.
Asking one another why
And hoping that God will provide an answer.

No one really knows
When the horrible nightmares will end.
Hopefully when the darkness ceases,
Sunlight will come shining through.

Because of this horrific attack
People are in shock and disbelief,
Realizing that the world has now
Lost all of its innocence.

MY TRAVELS

I've traveled all over.
I've traveled the land and the sky.
Been to places that hold memories
And have made many friends.

I've traveled by plane,
I've traveled by car,
I've even traveled by train,
And also I've traveled by boat.

I've seen cities and towns,
I've seen States and provinces aplenty.
I've seen many interesting people
And I've seen many historical sites as well.

But always at the end,
I love to come home the best.
For that's where friends and family are
And where I am known the best!

NOTHING TO LOSE

A lonely old man walking down the street
Who is bundled up even though it's warm.
Pushes a shopping cart filled with goods,
That he has collected from many garbage can long ago.

His sad pathetic face is dropping with age,
His eyes have lost the light that was once there.
A straight line now forms where his mouth had once
curved into a smile.
When you look at him you wonder what had once been there.

People rush to and fro,
Pretty much ignoring the lonely old man.
Occasionally he'll be taunted at by teenagers
But he'll ignore them and they go on by.

The lonely old man stops to rest.
People start to throw money at him.
He bends over to pick it up.
No one really looks at him.

An old lady stops by to help him.
As she helps him, she touches his hand.
They look at one another then
And it seems as if they are the only two people on the street.

The old lady smiles and so does the lonely old man.
She helps him stand up and she lets go of his hand.
"Thank you for your help," he said.
"Your welcome," she said, "When I looked at you it
made me realize that I had nothing
To lose but to see you smile."

ONLY IN THE PAST

My Grandmother loves to tell me
Stories about her past.
To hear her tell it that was the only way to do anything.
Although for me the past is a mystery.

This past she tells me
Started long before television or radio.
They only got around in carriages with horses driving,
Not vehicles that are noisy and take you from point a
to b.

Only in the past,
Did she walk so many miles to school.
She got an education in a one-room schoolhouse.
The teacher taught all the grades and every lesson,
Sometimes they were men or sometimes they were women.

In the past,
Families and friends got together and really enjoyed
themselves.
My Grandmother says they didn't have this thing
called peer pressure.

In the past
There were two World Wars.
My Grandmother hopes that there is never a third
And that no one she knows and loves is around in case
there is.
She doesn't want them to know what war can do.

Some part of the past was confusing
Like the 60's, 70's, and 80's.
When that was the present
She missed the good old days.
Now the 90's were just a continuation of the 80's, not
much change there.

As my Grandmother is always fond of saying
No matter what time you are in the present,
Remembering the past is good for it shows how far you
have come
And you can see all the people that you love around
you.
That is the best part, not everything is only in the past.

REMEMBERING PEARL HARBOR

Sixty years ago
On December 7, 1941,
At the Island of Oahu in Hawaii,
Pearl Harbor was attacked.

A quiet Sunday morning
It had started out to be,
But, one that quickly turned out to be
A nightmare that no one could fathom.

A once proud navy fleet
Reduced to nothing but rubble.
A memorial now stands where
The U.S.S. Arizona has been commemorated.

Many hearts were broken,
As they lost friends and comrades.
Not one person forgetting
The bravery that was shown during that day.

Time eventually healed most wounds
Life eventually continued on.
As each anniversary arrives on December 7,
Everyone remembers what happened at Pearl Harbor.

SECOND CHANCES

Second chances are starting a new beginning.

Second chances are forgetting about the past.

Second chances are accepting things that can't be changed in the past.

Second chances are setting a new course in life.

Second chances are learning to walk in the ways of the Lord.

Second chances are moving on from the mistakes and learning from them.

Second chances are learning to love yourself for the very first time.

Second chances are accepting who you are as a person.

And second chances are just sometimes those – second chances.

Live your life to the fullest!

THIS OLD HOUSE

Somewhere in the middle of no where
A house stand alone
With no one to keep it happy,
As they have left a long time ago.
Only the house has its memories.

You can picture the house during its younger days.
A family has lived there for its fairly big
One would have felt safe and comfortable
Inside its walls
For they have stood the test of time.

In its younger days
The house would have had a sunny disposition.
A lot of trees and flowers blooming the summer
With nature coming and going,
Nothing ever stays the same.

It had seen its share of people coming and going,
Seeing loved ones passing away,
And feeling the sadness in everyone's hearts.
Enjoying the many wonderful parties
And reveling in the quiet days.

It has stood the test of time,
Has felt loved by caring people,
And has shared all emotion.
For this old house
Has seen all and has enjoyed all.

THOUGHTS ON TURNING THIRTY

Midnight is fast approaching
Twelve chimes have just sounded
A new day has dawned,
Egad it's my 30th birthday.

As I look into the mirror,
I see that my facial features haven't changed.
Something that I am thankful for
That I don't have such a thing called "Crow's feet."

I don't know if it's good or bad
That when people look at me
They think that I look 18 or 22.
But, I suppose that's good, for when I'm 40 I'll look 30.

People say that 30 is not so bad
Although after all I've heard today
From my family and friends
I think I have changed my mind.

Embarking on a new decade
Excited for any changes that may come my way.
Hoping things turn out for the best.
These are just a few of my thoughts on turning 30.

WHEREVER I ROAM

No matter what life may bring
Or the challenges that I face,
It's wherever I roam
That I learn the lessons.

Wherever I roam,
I've had my ups and downs,
My light turn to darkness
Then my darkness turns to light.

However I may roam
It's the negatives that turn to positives
The sadness turned to happiness
And made the light shine down on me.

Wherever I roamed,
I learned the lessons handed down to me
For where I roam
They will stay with me forever.

Printed in the United States
47034LVS00002B/1-81